CONTENTS

TIME-HONORED CLASSICS

PIZZA MEAT LOAF

     1 envelope LIPTON® RECIPE SECRETS® Onion
          Soup Mix*
     2 pounds ground beef
  1½ cups fresh bread crumbs
     2 eggs
     1 small green bell pepper, chopped (optional)
    ¼ cup water
     1 cup RAGÚ® OLD WORLD STYLE® Pasta Sauce
     1 cup shredded mozzarella cheese (about 4 ounces)

Also terrific with LIPTON® RECIPE SECRETS® Savory Herb with Garlic Soup Mix.

1. Preheat oven to 350°F. In large bowl, combine all ingredients except ½ cup pasta sauce and ½ cup cheese.

2. In 13×9-inch baking or roasting pan, shape into loaf. Top with remaining ½ cup pasta sauce.

3. Bake uncovered 50 minutes.

4. Sprinkle top with remaining ½ cup cheese. Bake an additional 10 minutes or until done. Let stand 10 minutes before serving.   *Makes 8 servings*

Recipe Tip: When grating cheese, spray your box grater with nonstick cooking spray and place on a sheet of waxed paper. When you finish grating, clean-up is a breeze. Simply discard the waxed paper and rinse the grater clean.

SLOW COOKER STUFFED PEPPERS

1 pound ground beef
1 package (7 ounces) Spanish rice mix
½ cup diced celery
1 small onion, chopped
1 egg
4 medium green bell peppers, halved lengthwise, cored and seeded
1 can (28 ounces) whole peeled tomatoes, undrained
1 can (10¾ ounces) condensed tomato soup, undiluted
1 cup water

Slow Cooker Directions

1. Combine beef, rice mix (reserving seasoning packet), celery, onion and egg in large bowl. Divide meat mixture evenly among pepper halves.

2. Pour tomatoes with juice into slow cooker. Arrange filled pepper halves on top of tomatoes. Combine tomato soup, water and rice mix seasoning packet in large bowl. Pour over peppers. Cover and cook on LOW 8 to 10 hours.   *Makes 4 servings*

LIPTON® ONION BURGERS

1 envelope LIPTON® RECIPE SECRETS® Onion Soup Mix*
2 pounds ground beef
½ cup water

*Also terrific with LIPTON® RECIPE SECRETS® Beefy Onion, Onion Mushroom, Beefy Mushroom, Savory Herb with Garlic or Ranch Soup Mix.

1. In large bowl, combine all ingredients; shape into 8 patties.

2. Grill or broil until done.
          Makes about 8 servings

*Slow Cooker
Stuffed Peppers*

CONTADINA®
CLASSIC LASAGNE

1 pound dry lasagne noodles,
   cooked
1 tablespoon olive or
   vegetable oil
1 cup chopped onion
½ cup chopped green bell
   pepper
2 cloves garlic, minced
1½ pounds lean ground beef
2 cans (14.5 ounces each)
   CONTADINA® Recipe
   Ready Diced Tomatoes,
   undrained
1 can (8 ounces)
   CONTADINA Tomato
   Sauce
1 can (6 ounces)
   CONTADINA Tomato
   Paste
½ cup dry red wine or beef
   broth
1½ teaspoons salt
1 teaspoon dried oregano
   leaves, crushed
1 teaspoon dried basil leaves,
   crushed
½ teaspoon ground black
   pepper
1 egg
1 cup (8 ounces) ricotta
   cheese
2 cups (8 ounces) shredded
   mozzarella cheese,
   divided

1. Cook pasta according to package directions; drain.

2. Meanwhile, heat oil in large skillet. Add onion, bell pepper and garlic; sauté for 3 minutes or until vegetables are tender.

3. Add beef; cook for 5 to 6 minutes or until evenly browned.

4. Add tomatoes with juice, tomato sauce, tomato paste, wine, salt, oregano, basil and black pepper; bring to a boil. Reduce heat to low; simmer, uncovered, for 20 minutes, stirring occasionally.

5. Beat egg slightly in medium bowl. Stir in ricotta cheese and 1 cup mozzarella cheese.

6. Layer noodles, half of meat sauce, noodles, all of ricotta cheese mixture, noodles and remaining meat sauce in ungreased 13×9-inch baking dish. Sprinkle with remaining mozzarella cheese.

7. Bake in preheated 350°F oven for 25 to 30 minutes or until heated through. Let stand for 10 minutes before cutting to serve. *Makes 10 servings*

Prep Time: 35 minutes
Cook Time: 30 minutes
Standing Time: 10 minutes

SAUCY STUFFED PEPPERS

6 medium green bell peppers
1¼ cups water
  2 cups low-sodium tomato
    juice, divided
  1 can (6 ounces) tomato
    paste
  1 teaspoon dried oregano
    leaves, crushed, divided
½ teaspoon dried basil leaves,
    crushed
½ teaspoon garlic powder,
    divided
  1 pound lean ground beef
1½ cups QUAKER® Oats (quick
    or old fashioned,
    uncooked)
  1 medium tomato, chopped
¼ cup chopped carrot
¼ cup chopped onion

Heat oven to 350°F. Cut peppers lengthwise in half. Remove membranes and seeds; set peppers aside. In large saucepan, combine water, 1 cup tomato juice, tomato paste, ½ teaspoon oregano, basil and ¼ teaspoon garlic powder. Simmer 10 to 15 minutes.

Combine beef, oats, remaining 1 cup tomato juice, ½ teaspoon oregano and ¼ teaspoon garlic powder with tomato, carrot and onion; mix well. Fill each pepper half with about ⅓ cup meat mixture. Place in 13×9-inch glass baking dish; pour sauce evenly over peppers. Bake 45 to 50 minutes.

Makes 12 servings

TEMPTING TACO BURGERS

1 envelope LIPTON® RECIPE
    SECRETS® Onion-
    Mushroom Soup Mix*
1 pound ground beef
½ cup chopped tomato
¼ cup finely chopped green
    bell pepper
1 teaspoon chili powder
¼ cup water

Also terrific with LIPTON® RECIPE SECRETS® Onion, Beefy Onion or Beefy Mushroom Soup Mix.

1. In large bowl, combine all ingredients; shape into 4 patties.

2. Grill or broil until done. Serve, if desired, on hamburger buns and top with shredded lettuce and Cheddar cheese.

Makes 4 servings

Recipe Tip: The best way to test for doneness of beef, pork, fish and poultry is to use a meat thermometer or an instant read thermometer. But, you may want to try this quick touch test first: Gently press a piece of uncooked flesh to feel what rare feels like; the flesh will become tighter and more resistant as it cooks. Medium will have some give; well-done will be quite firm.

LASAGNA SUPREME

8 ounces uncooked lasagna
   noodles
½ pound ground beef
½ pound mild Italian
   sausage, casings removed
1 medium onion, chopped
2 cloves garlic, minced
1 can (14½ ounces) whole
   peeled tomatoes,
   undrained and chopped
1 can (6 ounces) tomato
   paste
2 teaspoons dried basil
   leaves
1 teaspoon dried marjoram
   leaves
1 can (4 ounces) sliced
   mushrooms, drained
2 eggs
2 cups (16 ounces) cream-
   style cottage cheese
¾ cup grated Parmesan
   cheese, divided
2 tablespoons dried parsley
   flakes
½ teaspoon salt
½ teaspoon black pepper
2 cups (8 ounces) shredded
   Cheddar cheese
3 cups (12 ounces) shredded
   mozzarella cheese

1. Cook lasagna noodles according to package directions; drain.

2. Cook meats, onion and garlic in large skillet over medium-high heat until meat is brown, stirring to separate meat. Drain drippings from skillet.

3. Add tomatoes with juice, tomato paste, basil and marjoram. Reduce heat to low. Cover; simmer 15 minutes, stirring often. Stir in mushrooms; set aside.

4. Preheat oven to 375°F. Beat eggs in large bowl; add cottage cheese, ½ cup Parmesan cheese, parsley, salt and pepper. Mix well.

5. Place half the noodles in bottom of greased 13×9-inch baking pan. Spread half the cottage cheese mixture over noodles, then half the meat mixture and half the Cheddar cheese and mozzarella cheese. Repeat layers. Sprinkle with remaining ¼ cup Parmesan cheese.

6. Bake lasagna 40 to 45 minutes or until bubbly. Let stand 10 minutes before cutting.
Makes 8 to 10 servings

Note: Lasagna may be assembled, covered and refrigerated up to 2 days in advance. Bake, uncovered, in preheated 375°F oven 60 minutes or until bubbly.

Lasagna Supreme

Choice Casseroles

Tacos in Pasta Shells

    1 package (3 ounces) cream cheese with chives
   18 jumbo pasta shells
1¼ pounds ground beef
    1 teaspoon salt
    1 teaspoon chili powder
    2 tablespoons butter, melted
    1 cup prepared taco sauce
    1 cup (4 ounces) shredded Cheddar cheese
    1 cup (4 ounces) shredded Monterey Jack cheese
1½ cups crushed tortilla chips
    1 cup sour cream
    3 green onions, chopped

1. Cut cream cheese into ½-inch cubes. Let stand at room temperature until softened. Cook pasta according to package directions. Place in colander and rinse under warm running water. Drain well. Return to saucepan.

2. Preheat oven to 350°F. Butter 13×9-inch baking pan. Cook beef in large skillet over medium-high heat until brown, stirring to separate meat; drain drippings. Reduce heat to medium-low. Add cream cheese, salt and chili powder; simmer 5 minutes.

3. Toss shells with butter. Fill shells with beef mixture using spoon. Arrange shells in prepared pan. Pour taco sauce over each shell. Cover with foil.

4. Bake 15 minutes. Uncover; top with cheeses and chips. Bake 15 minutes more or until bubbly. Top with sour cream-and onions. Garnish, if desired.

Makes 4 to 6 servings

BEEF STROGANOFF CASSEROLE

  1 pound lean ground beef
  ¼ teaspoon salt
  ⅛ teaspoon black pepper
  1 teaspoon vegetable oil
  8 ounces sliced mushrooms
  1 large onion, chopped
  3 cloves garlic, minced
  ¼ cup dry white wine
  1 can (10¾ ounces)
      condensed cream of
      mushroom soup,
      undiluted
  ½ cup sour cream
  1 tablespoon Dijon mustard
  4 cups cooked egg noodles
      Chopped fresh parsley
      (optional)

Preheat oven to 350°F. Spray 13×9-inch baking dish with nonstick cooking spray.

Place beef in large skillet; season with salt and pepper. Brown beef over medium-high heat until no longer pink, stirring to separate beef. Drain fat from skillet; set beef aside.

Heat oil in same skillet over medium-high heat until hot. Add mushrooms, onion and garlic; cook and stir 2 minutes or until onion is tender. Add wine. Reduce heat to medium-low and simmer 3 minutes. Remove from heat; stir in soup, sour cream and mustard until well combined. Return beef to skillet.

Place noodles in prepared dish. Pour beef mixture over noodles; stir until noodles are well coated.

Bake, uncovered, 30 minutes or until heated through. Sprinkle with parsley, if desired.

Makes 6 servings

HEARTLAND SHEPHERD'S PIE

  ¾ pound ground beef
  1 medium onion, chopped
  1 can (14½ ounces) DEL
      MONTE® Original Recipe
      Stewed Tomatoes
  1 can (8 ounces) DEL
      MONTE Tomato Sauce
  1 can (14½ ounces) DEL
      MONTE Mixed
      Vegetables, drained
    Instant mashed potato
      flakes plus ingredients to
      prepare
  3 cloves garlic, minced

1. Preheat oven to 375°F. In large skillet, brown meat and onion over medium-high heat; drain. Add tomatoes and tomato sauce; cook over high heat until thickened, stirring frequently. Stir in mixed vegetables. Season with salt and pepper, if desired.

2. Spoon into 2-quart baking dish; set aside. Prepare 6 servings mashed potatoes according to package directions, first cooking garlic in specified amount of butter.

3. Top meat mixture with potatoes. Bake 20 minutes or until heated through.

Makes 4 to 6 servings

Beef Stroganoff Casserole

SPINACH-POTATO BAKE

1 pound extra-lean
    (90% lean) ground beef
½ cup sliced fresh
    mushrooms
1 small onion, chopped
2 cloves garlic, minced
1 package (10 ounces) frozen
    chopped spinach,
    thawed, well drained
½ teaspoon ground nutmeg
1 pound russet potatoes,
    peeled, cooked, mashed
¼ cup light sour cream
¼ cup fat-free (skim) milk
    Salt and black pepper
½ cup (2 ounces) shredded
    Cheddar cheese

Preheat oven to 400°F. Spray deep 9-inch casserole dish with nonstick cooking spray.

Brown ground beef in large skillet. Drain. Add mushrooms, onion and garlic; cook until tender. Stir in spinach and nutmeg; cover. Heat thoroughly, stirring occasionally.

Combine potatoes, sour cream and milk. Add to ground beef mixture; season with salt and pepper to taste. Spoon into prepared casserole dish; sprinkle with cheese.

Bake 15 to 20 minutes or until slightly puffed and cheese is melted.   *Makes 6 servings*

MALAYSIAN CURRIED BEEF

2 tablespoons vegetable oil
2 large onions, chopped
1 piece fresh ginger (about
    1 inch square), minced
2 cloves garlic, minced
2 tablespoons curry powder
1 teaspoon salt
2 large baking potatoes
    (1 pound), peeled and
    cut into chunks
1 cup beef broth
1 pound ground beef chuck
2 ripe tomatoes (12 ounces),
    peeled and cut into
    chunks
    Hot cooked rice

1. Heat wok over medium-high heat 1 minute or until hot. Drizzle oil into wok and heat 30 seconds. Add onions and stir-fry 2 minutes. Add ginger, garlic, curry and salt to wok. Cook and stir about 1 minute or until fragrant. Add potatoes; cook and stir 2 to 3 minutes. Add beef broth to potato mixture. Cover and bring to a boil. Reduce heat to low; simmer about 20 minutes or until potatoes are fork-tender.

2. Stir ground beef into potato mixture. Cook and stir about 5 minutes or until beef is browned and no pink remains; spoon off fat if necessary.

3. Add tomato chunks and stir gently until thoroughly heated. Spoon beef mixture into serving dish. Top center with rice.
Makes 4 servings

PASTA "PIZZA"

3 eggs, slightly beaten
½ cup milk
2 cups corkscrew macaroni,
   cooked and drained
½ cup (2 ounces) shredded
   Wisconsin Cheddar
   cheese
¼ cup finely chopped onion
1 pound lean ground beef
1 can (15 ounces) tomato
   sauce
1 teaspoon dried basil leaves
1 teaspoon dried oregano
   leaves
½ teaspoon garlic salt
1 medium tomato, thinly
   sliced
1 green pepper, sliced into
   rings
1½ cups (6 ounces) shredded
   Wisconsin Mozzarella
   cheese

Combine eggs and milk in small bowl. Add to hot macaroni; mix lightly to coat. Stir in Cheddar cheese and onion; mix well. Spread macaroni mixture onto bottom of well-buttered 14-inch pizza pan. Bake at 350°F, 25 minutes. Meanwhile, in large skillet over medium-high heat, brown meat, stirring occasionally to separate meat; drain. Stir in tomato sauce, basil, oregano and garlic salt. Spoon over macaroni crust. Arrange tomato slices and pepper rings on top. Sprinkle with Mozzarella cheese. Continue baking 15 minutes or until cheese is bubbly. *Makes 8 servings*

*Favorite recipe from **Wisconsin Milk Marketing Board***

ZUCCHINI LASAGNE

3 cans (8 ounces each)
   CONTADINA® Tomato
   Sauce
1 can (14.5 ounces)
   CONTADINA Stewed
   Tomatoes, undrained
1 teaspoon granulated sugar
1 teaspoon Italian herb
   seasoning
1 teaspoon black pepper
1 pound lean ground beef
3 teaspoon seasoned salt
6 medium zucchini squash,
   sliced ⅛ inch thick
2 cups (8 ounces) shredded
   mozzarella cheese
2 cups (15 ounces) ricotta
   cheese
3 tablespoons grated
   Parmesan cheese

1. Combine tomato sauce, stewed tomatoes, sugar, Italian seasoning and pepper in saucepan.

2. Simmer, uncovered, for 25 minutes, stirring occasionally. In medium skillet, brown beef; drain. Stir in seasoned salt and tomato sauce mixture.

3. Butter bottom of 13×9-inch baking dish. Layer half of zucchini slices on bottom of baking dish; sprinkle with salt. Spread half of ground beef mixture over zucchini. Sprinkle with mozzarella cheese and ricotta cheese. Repeat with zucchini and beef layer. Sprinkle Parmesan cheese on top. Bake in preheated 350°F oven for 45 minutes. *Makes 8 cups*

BEEFY NACHO CRESCENT BAKE

1 pound lean ground beef
½ cup chopped onion
¼ teaspoon salt
⅛ teaspoon black pepper
1 tablespoon chili powder
1 teaspoon ground cumin
1 teaspoon dried oregano
   leaves
1 can (11 ounces) condensed
   nacho cheese soup,
   undiluted
1 cup milk
1 can (8 ounces) refrigerated
   crescent roll dough
¼ cup (1 ounce) shredded
   Cheddar cheese
   Chopped fresh cilantro
   (optional)
   Salsa (optional)

Preheat oven to 375°F. Spray
13×9-inch baking dish with
nonstick cooking spray.

Place beef and onion in large
skillet; season with salt and
pepper. Brown beef over
medium-high heat until no
longer pink, stirring to separate
meat. Drain fat. Stir in chili
powder, cumin and oregano.
Cook and stir 2 minutes; remove
from heat.

Combine soup and milk in
medium bowl, stirring until
smooth. Pour soup mixture into
prepared dish, spreading evenly.

Separate crescent dough into
4 rectangles; press perforations
together firmly. Roll each
rectangle to 8×4 inches.

Cut each rectangle in half
crosswise to form 8 (4-inch)
squares.

Spoon about ¼ cup beef mixture
in center of each square. Lift
4 corners of dough up over filling
to meet in center; pinch and twist
firmly to seal. Place squares in
dish.

Bake, uncovered, 20 to
25 minutes or until crusts are
golden brown. Sprinkle cheese
over squares. Bake 5 minutes or
until cheese melts. To serve,
spoon soup mixture in dish over
each serving; sprinkle with
cilantro, if desired. Serve with
salsa, if desired.

Makes 4 servings

*Beefy Nacho Crescent
Bake*

SHEPHERD'S PIE

1⅓ cups instant mashed potato
    buds
1⅔ cups milk
  2 tablespoons margarine or
    butter
  1 teaspoon salt, divided
  1 pound ground beef
 ¼ teaspoon black pepper
  1 jar (12 ounces) beef gravy
  1 package (10 ounces) frozen
    mixed vegetables,
    thawed and drained
 ¾ cup grated Parmesan
    cheese

1. Preheat broiler. Prepare
4 servings of mashed potatoes
according to package directions
using milk, margarine and
½ teaspoon salt.

2. While mashed potatoes are
cooking, brown meat in medium
broilerproof skillet over medium-
high heat, stirring to separate
meat. Drain drippings. Sprinkle
meat with remaining ½ teaspoon
salt and pepper. Add gravy and
vegetables; mix well. Cook over
medium-low heat 5 minutes or
until hot.

3. Spoon prepared potatoes
around outside edge of skillet,
leaving 3-inch circle in center.
Sprinkle cheese evenly over
potatoes. Broil 4 to 5 inches from
heat source 3 minutes or until
cheese is golden brown and meat
mixture is bubbly.

Makes 4 servings

Prep and Cook Time:
28 minutes

CLASSIC HAMBURGER CASSEROLE

  1 pound ground beef
  1 package (9 ounces) frozen
    cut green beans, thawed
    and drained
  1 can (10¾ ounces)
    condensed tomato soup
 ¼ cup water
 ½ teaspoon seasoned salt
 ⅛ teaspoon pepper
  2 cups hot mashed potatoes
1⅓ cups *French's®* French
    Fried Onions, divided
 ½ cup (2 ounces) shredded
    Cheddar cheese

Preheat oven to 350°F. In medium
skillet, brown ground beef; drain.
Stir in green beans, soup, water
and seasonings; pour into
1½-quart casserole. In medium
bowl, combine mashed potatoes
and ⅔ *cup* French Fried Onions.
Spoon potato mixture in mounds
around edge of casserole. Bake,
uncovered, at 350°F for
25 minutes or until heated
through. Top potatoes with
cheese and remaining ⅔ *cup*
onions; bake, uncovered,
5 minutes or until onions are
golden brown.

Makes 4 to 6 servings

Shepherd's Pie

STRING PIE

1 pound ground beef
½ cup chopped onion
¼ cup chopped green pepper
1 jar (15½ ounces) spaghetti
   sauce
8 ounces spaghetti, cooked
   and drained
⅓ cup grated Parmesan
   cheese
2 eggs, beaten
2 teaspoons butter
1 cup cottage cheese
½ cup (2 ounces) shredded
   mozzarella cheese

Preheat oven to 350°F. Cook beef, onion and green pepper in large skillet over medium-high heat until meat is browned. Drain fat. Stir in spaghetti sauce. Combine spaghetti, Parmesan cheese, eggs and butter in large bowl; mix well. Place in bottom of 13×9-inch baking pan. Spread cottage cheese over top; cover with sauce mixture. Sprinkle with mozzarella cheese. Bake until mixture is thoroughly heated and cheese is melted, about 20 minutes.

Makes 6 to 8 servings

*Favorite recipe from **North Dakota Beef Commission***

RANCH LENTIL CASSEROLE

2 cups lentils, rinsed
4 cups water
1 pound lean ground beef
1 cup water
1 cup ketchup
1 envelope dry onion soup
   mix
1 teaspoon prepared
   mustard
1 teaspoon vinegar

Cook lentils in 4 cups water for 30 minutes. Drain. Brown ground beef. Combine lentils, beef, 1 cup water and remaining ingredients in baking dish. Bake at 400°F for 30 minutes.

Makes 8 servings

Note: Prepared recipe can be frozen.

*Favorite recipe from **USA Dry Pea & Lentil Council***

String Pie

MOUSSAKA

1 large eggplant
2½ teaspoons salt, divided
2 large zucchini
2 large russet potatoes,
    peeled
½ cup olive oil, divided
1½ pounds ground beef or
    lamb
1 large onion, chopped
2 cloves garlic, minced
1 cup chopped tomatoes
½ cup dry red or white wine
¼ cup chopped fresh parsley
¼ teaspoon ground cinnamon
⅛ teaspoon black pepper
1 cup grated Parmesan
    cheese, divided
4 tablespoons butter or
    margarine, divided
⅓ cup all-purpose flour
¼ teaspoon ground nutmeg
2 cups milk

Cut eggplant lengthwise into
½-inch-thick slices. Place in large
colander; sprinkle with
1 teaspoon salt. Drain 30 minutes.
Cut zucchini lengthwise into
⅜-inch-thick slices. Cut potatoes
lengthwise into ¼-inch-thick
slices.

Heat ¼ cup oil in large skillet
over medium heat until hot. Add
potatoes in single layer. Cook
5 minutes per side or until tender
and lightly browned. Remove
potatoes from skillet; drain on
paper towels. Add more oil to
skillet, if needed. Cook zucchini
2 minutes per side or until
tender. Drain on paper towels.
Add more oil to skillet. Cook
eggplant 5 minutes per side or
until tender. Drain on paper
towels. Drain oil from skillet;
discard.

Heat skillet over medium-high
heat just until hot. Add beef,
onion and garlic; cook and stir
5 minutes or until meat is no
longer pink. Pour off drippings.
Stir in tomatoes, wine, parsley,
1 teaspoon salt, cinnamon and
pepper. Bring to a boil over high
heat. Reduce heat to low. Simmer
10 minutes or until liquid is
evaporated.

Preheat oven to 325°F. Grease
13×9-inch baking dish. Arrange
potatoes in bottom; sprinkle with
¼ cup cheese. Top with zucchini
and ¼ cup cheese, then eggplant
and ¼ cup cheese. Spoon meat
mixture over top.

To prepare sauce, melt butter in
medium saucepan over low heat.
Blend in flour, remaining
½ teaspoon salt and nutmeg with
wire whisk. Cook 1 minute,
whisking constantly. Gradually
whisk in milk. Cook over medium
heat, until mixture boils and
thickens, whisking constantly.
Pour sauce evenly over meat
mixture in dish; sprinkle with
remaining ¼ cup cheese. Bake
30 to 40 minutes or until hot and
bubbly. Garnish as desired.
Makes 6 to 8 servings

STUFFED MEXICAN PIZZA PIE

1 pound ground beef
1 large onion, chopped
1 large green bell pepper, chopped
1½ cups UNCLE BEN'S® Instant Rice
2 cans (14½ ounces each) Mexican-style stewed tomatoes, undrained
2 cups (8 ounces) shredded Mexican-style seasoned Monterey Jack-Colby cheese blend, divided
1 container (10 ounces) refrigerated pizza crust dough

1. Preheat oven to 425°F. Spray 13×9-inch baking pan with cooking spray; set aside.

2. Spray large nonstick skillet with nonstick cooking spray; heat over high heat until hot. Add beef, onion and bell pepper; cook and stir 5 minutes or until meat is no longer pink.

3. Add rice, stewed tomatoes and ⅔ cup water. Bring to a boil. Pour beef mixture into prepared baking pan. Sprinkle with 1¼ cups cheese and stir until blended.

4. Unroll pizza crust dough on work surface. Place dough in one even layer over mixture in baking pan. Cut 6 to 8 slits in dough with sharp knife. Bake 10 minutes or until crust is lightly browned. Sprinkle top of crust with remaining ¾ cup cheese;

continue baking 4 minutes or until cheese is melted and crust is deep golden brown. Let stand 5 minutes before cutting.

Makes 6 servings

MEXICAN STUFFED SHELLS

12 pasta stuffing shells, cooked and drained
1 pound ground beef
1 jar (12 ounces) mild or medium picante sauce
½ cup water
1 can (8 ounces) tomato sauce
1 can (4 ounces) chopped green chilies, drained
1 cup (4 ounces) shredded Monterey Jack cheese, divided
1⅓ cups *French's*® French Fried Onions

Preheat oven to 350°F. In large skillet, brown ground beef; drain. In small bowl, combine picante sauce, water and tomato sauce. Stir ½ cup sauce mixture into beef along with chilies, ½ cup cheese and ⅔ *cup* French Fried Onions; mix well. Spread half the remaining sauce mixture in bottom of 10-inch round baking dish. Stuff cooked shells with beef mixture. Arrange shells in baking dish; top with remaining sauce. Bake, covered, at 350°F for 30 minutes or until heated through. Top with remaining ⅔ *cup* onions and cheese; bake, uncovered, 5 minutes or until cheese is melted.

Makes 6 servings

TAMALE PIE

1 tablespoon olive or
  vegetable oil
1 small onion, chopped
1 pound ground beef
1 envelope LIPTON® RECIPE
  SECRETS® Onion Soup
  Mix*
1 can (14½ ounces) stewed
  tomatoes, undrained
½ cup water
1 can (15 to 19 ounces) red
  kidney beans, rinsed and
  drained
1 package (8½ ounces) corn
  muffin mix

*Also terrific with LIPTON® RECIPE
SECRETS® Fiesta Herb with Red
Pepper, Onion-Mushroom, Beefy Onion
or Beefy Mushroom Soup Mix.*

• Preheat oven to 400°F.

• In 12-inch skillet, heat oil over
medium heat and cook onion,
stirring occasionally, 3 minutes or
until tender. Stir in ground beef
and cook until browned.

• Stir in onion soup mix blended
with tomatoes and water. Bring to
a boil over high heat, stirring
with spoon to crush tomatoes.
Reduce heat to low and stir in
beans. Simmer uncovered,
stirring occasionally, 10 minutes.
Turn into 2-quart casserole.

• Prepare corn muffin mix
according to package directions.
Spoon evenly over casserole.

• Bake uncovered 15 minutes or
until corn topping is golden and
filling is hot.

Makes about 6 servings

BAKED PASTA CASSEROLE

1½ cups (3 ounces) uncooked
  wagon wheel or rotelle
  pasta
3 ounces 95% lean ground
  beef sirloin
2 tablespoons chopped onion
2 tablespoons chopped green
  bell pepper
1 clove garlic, minced
½ cup fat-free spaghetti
  sauce
  Black pepper
2 tablespoons shredded
  Italian-style mozzarella
  and Parmesan cheese
  blend
  Pepperoncini (optional)

1. Preheat oven to 350°F. Cook
pasta according to package
directions; drain. Return pasta to
saucepan.

2. Meanwhile, heat small
nonstick skillet over medium-
high heat. Add beef, onion, bell
pepper and garlic; cook and stir
3 to 4 minutes or until beef is
browned and vegetables are
crisp-tender. Drain.

3. Add beef mixture, spaghetti
sauce and black pepper to pasta
in saucepan; mix well. Spoon
mixture into 1-quart baking dish.
Sprinkle with cheese.

4. Bake 15 minutes or until
heated through. Serve with
pepperoncini, if desired.

Makes 2 servings

Tamale Pie

MEXICAN LASAGNA

1 package (16 sheets)
BARILLA® Oven Ready
Lasagna Noodles (do not
boil)
1 pound ground beef
1 package (1.5 ounces) taco
seasoning
1 jar (26 ounces) BARILLA®
Lasagna & Casserole
Sauce or Marinara Pasta
Sauce
2 eggs
1 container (15 ounces)
ricotta cheese
4 cups (16 ounces) shredded
Mexican-style cheese,
divided

1. Preheat oven to 375°F. Spray
13×9×2-inch baking pan with
nonstick cooking spray. Remove
12 lasagna noodles from package.
Do not boil.

2. Cook ground beef and taco
seasoning in large skillet,
following directions on seasoning
package. Remove from heat; stir
in lasagna sauce.

3. Beat eggs in medium bowl.
Stir in ricotta cheese and 2 cups
Mexican-style cheese.

4. To assemble lasagna, spread
1 cup meat mixture over bottom
of pan. Arrange 4 uncooked
lasagna noodles over meat
mixture, overlapping edges if
necessary to fit pan. Top with half
of ricotta mixture and 1 cup meat
mixture. Repeat layers
(4 uncooked lasagna noodles,
remaining half of ricotta mixture

and 1 cup meat mixture); top
with remaining 4 uncooked
lasagna noodles, remaining meat
mixture and remaining 2 cups
Mexican-style cheese.

5. Cover with foil and bake
45 to 55 minutes or until bubbly.
Uncover and continue cooking
about 5 minutes or until cheese is
melted. Let stand 15 minutes
before cutting.

Makes 12 servings

MONTEREY BLACK BEAN TORTILLA SUPPER

1 pound ground beef,
browned and drained
1½ cups bottled salsa
1 (15-ounce) can black
beans, drained
4 (8-inch) flour tortillas
2 cups (8 ounces) shredded
Wisconsin Monterey Jack
cheese*

**For authentic Mexican flavor,
substitute 2 cups shredded Wisconsin
Queso Blanco.*

Heat oven to 400°F. Combine
ground beef, salsa and beans. In
lightly greased 2-quart round
casserole, layer one tortilla,
⅔ cup meat mixture and ½ cup
cheese. Repeat layers three times.
Bake 30 minutes or until heated
through.

Makes 5 to 6 servings

*Favorite recipe from **Wisconsin Milk
Marketing Board***

Mexican Lasagna

Best Skillet Dishes

Chuckwagon BBQ Rice Round-Up

1 pound lean ground beef
1 (6.8-ounce) package RICE-A-RONI® Beef Flavor
2 tablespoons margarine or butter
2 cups frozen corn
½ cup prepared barbecue sauce
½ cup (2 ounces) shredded Cheddar cheese

1. In large skillet over medium-high heat, brown ground beef until well cooked. Remove from skillet; drain. Set aside.

2. In same skillet over medium heat, sauté rice-vermicelli mix with margarine until vermicelli is golden brown.

3. Slowly stir in 2½ cups water, corn and Special Seasonings; bring to a boil. Reduce heat to low. Cover; simmer 15 to 20 minutes or until rice is tender.

4. Stir in barbecue sauce and ground beef. Sprinkle with cheese. Cover; let stand 3 to 5 minutes or until cheese is melted. *Makes 4 servings*

Tip: Salsa can be substituted for barbecue sauce.

Prep Time: 5 minutes
Cook Time: 25 minutes

RAGÚ® CHILI MAC

1 tablespoon olive or
    vegetable oil
1 medium green bell pepper,
    chopped
1 pound ground beef
1 jar (26 to 28 ounces)
    RAGÚ® Old World Style®
    Pasta Sauce
2 tablespoons chili powder
8 ounces elbow macaroni,
    cooked and drained

1. In 12-inch nonstick skillet, heat oil over medium-high heat and cook green bell pepper, stirring occasionally, 3 minutes. Add ground beef and brown, stirring occasionally; drain.

2. Stir in Ragú Pasta Sauce and chili powder. Bring to a boil over high heat. Reduce heat to low and simmer covered 10 minutes.

3. Stir in macaroni and heat through. Serve, if desired, with sour cream and shredded Cheddar cheese.

Makes 4 servings

Prep Time: 10 minutes
Cook Time: 25 minutes

JOE'S SPECIAL

1 pound lean ground beef
2 cups sliced mushrooms
1 small onion, chopped
2 teaspoons Worcestershire
    sauce
1 teaspoon dried oregano
    leaves
1 teaspoon ground nutmeg
½ teaspoon garlic powder
½ teaspoon salt
1 package (10 ounces) frozen
    chopped spinach, thawed
4 large eggs, lightly beaten
⅓ cup grated Parmesan
    cheese

1. Spray large skillet with nonstick cooking spray. Add ground beef, mushrooms and onion; cook over medium-high heat 6 to 8 minutes or until onion is tender, breaking beef apart with wooden spoon. Add Worcestershire, oregano, nutmeg, garlic powder and salt. Cook until meat is no longer pink.

2. Drain spinach (do not squeeze dry); stir into meat mixture. Push mixture to one side of pan. Reduce heat to medium. Pour eggs into other side of pan; cook, without stirring, 1 to 2 minutes or until set on bottom. Lift eggs to allow uncooked portion to flow underneath. Repeat until softly set. Gently stir into meat mixture and heat through. Stir in cheese.

Makes 4 to 6 servings

Ragú® Chili Mac

ITALIAN BEEF BURRITO

1½ pounds ground beef
2 medium onions, finely chopped
2 medium red and/or green bell peppers, chopped
1 jar (26 to 28 ounces) RAGÚ® Robusto!™ Pasta Sauce
½ teaspoon dried oregano leaves, crushed
8 (10-inch) flour tortillas, warmed
2 cups shredded mozzarella cheese (about 8 ounces)

1. In 12-inch skillet, brown ground beef over medium-high heat.

2. Stir in onions and red bell peppers and cook, stirring occasionally, 5 minutes or until tender; drain. Stir in Ragú Pasta Sauce and oregano; heat through.

3. To serve, top each tortilla with ¼ cup cheese and 1 cup ground beef mixture; roll up and serve. *Makes 8 servings*

Prep Time: 15 minutes
Cook Time: 15 minutes

GREEK BEEF & RICE

1 bag SUCCESS® Rice
1 pound lean ground beef
2 medium zucchini, sliced
½ cup chopped onion
1 medium clove garlic, minced
1 can (14½ ounces) tomato sauce
¾ teaspoon dried basil leaves, crushed
¾ teaspoon salt
¼ teaspoon pepper

Prepare rice according to package directions.

Brown beef in large skillet, stirring occasionally to separate beef. Pour off all but 2 tablespoons drippings. Add zucchini, onion and garlic to skillet; cook and stir until crisp-tender. Add all remaining ingredients *except* rice; cover. Simmer 10 minutes, stirring occasionally. Add rice; heat thoroughly, stirring occasionally. Garnish, if desired.

Makes 6 servings

Italian Beef Burrito

QUICK GREEK PITAS

1 pound ground beef
1 package (10 ounces) frozen chopped spinach, thawed and well drained
4 green onions, chopped
1 can (2¼ ounces) sliced black olives, drained
1 teaspoon dried oregano, divided
¼ teaspoon black pepper
1 large tomato, diced
1 cup plain nonfat yogurt
½ cup mayonnaise
6 (6-inch) pita breads, warmed
Lettuce leaves
1 cup (4 ounces) crumbled feta cheese

Cook and stir ground beef in large skillet over medium-high heat until crumbly and no longer pink. Drain off drippings. Add spinach, green onions, olives, ½ teaspoon oregano and pepper; cook and stir 2 minutes. Stir in tomato.

Combine yogurt, mayonnaise and remaining ½ teaspoon oregano in small bowl. Split open pita breads; line each with lettuce leaf. Stir cheese into beef mixture and divide among pita pockets. Serve with yogurt sauce.

Makes 6 servings

SZECHWAN BEEF

1 pound ground beef
1 tablespoon vegetable oil
1 cup sliced carrots
1 cup frozen peas
⅓ cup water
3 tablespoons soy sauce
2 tablespoons cornstarch
¼ teaspoon ground ginger
1 jar (7 ounces) baby corn
1 medium onion, thinly sliced
Sliced mushrooms and olives as desired
¼ cup shredded Cheddar cheese
1⅓ cups uncooked instant rice

1. In wok or large skillet, brown ground beef; remove from wok; drain fat. Set aside.

2. Add oil to wok or skillet and return to medium heat. Add carrots and peas and stir-fry about 3 minutes.

3. In small cup combine water and soy sauce with cornstarch and ginger. Add to vegetables in wok.

4. Return ground beef to wok along with baby corn, onion, mushrooms, olives and cheese. Cook over medium heat until all ingredients are heated through.

5. Prepare instant rice according to package directions. Serve beef and vegetables over rice. *Makes 4 to 5 servings*

*Favorite recipe from **North Dakota Beef Commission***

PASTA BEEF & ZUCCHINI DINNER

1 pound extra lean ground beef
1 medium onion, chopped
1 clove garlic, crushed
½ teaspoon salt
2 (14-ounce) cans ready-to-serve beef broth
1 teaspoon Italian seasoning
¼ teaspoon crushed red pepper
2 cups uncooked mini lasagna or rotini pasta
2 cups sliced zucchini (cut ⅜ inch thick)
1 tablespoon cornstarch
¼ cup water
3 plum tomatoes, each cut into 4 wedges
2 tablespoons grated Parmesan cheese

In large nonstick skillet, cook ground beef with onion, garlic and salt over medium heat 8 to 10 minutes or until beef is browned, stirring occasionally to break up beef into 1-inch crumbles. Remove beef mixture with slotted spoon; pour off drippings. Set aside.

Add broth, Italian seasoning and red pepper to same skillet. Bring to a boil; add pasta. Reduce heat to medium; simmer, uncovered, for 6 minutes, stirring occasionally. Add zucchini; continue cooking for an additional 6 to 8 minutes or until pasta is tender, yet firm. Push pasta and zucchini to side of skillet. Mix cornstarch with water and add to broth in skillet; bring to a boil. Return beef mixture to skillet. Add tomatoes; heat through, stirring occasionally. Spoon into serving dish; sprinkle with Parmesan cheese.

Makes 5 servings

*Favorite recipe from **North Dakota Wheat Commission***

CHEESEBURGER MACARONI

1 cup mostaccioli or elbow macaroni, uncooked
1 pound ground beef
1 medium onion, chopped
1 can (14½ ounces) DEL MONTE® Diced Tomatoes with Basil, Garlic & Oregano
¼ cup DEL MONTE Tomato Ketchup
1 cup (4 ounces) shredded Cheddar cheese

1. Cook pasta according to package directions; drain.

2. Brown meat with onion in large skillet; drain. Season with salt and pepper, if desired. Stir in undrained tomatoes, ketchup and pasta; heat through.

3. Top with cheese. Garnish, if desired. *Makes 4 servings*

Prep Time: 8 minutes
Cook Time: 15 minutes

TEX-MEX BEEF & BLACK BEAN SKILLET

1 pound lean ground beef
1 medium onion, chopped
2 cloves garlic, minced
1 tablespoon Mexican seasoning*
1 (6.8-ounce) package RICE-A-RONI® Spanish Rice
2 tablespoons margarine or butter
1 (16-ounce) jar salsa
1 (16-ounce) can black beans, rinsed and drained
1 cup shredded Monterey Jack cheese

*1 teaspoon chili powder, 1 teaspoon ground cumin, 1 teaspoon garlic salt and ¼ teaspoon cayenne pepper may be substituted.

1. In large skillet over medium-high heat, cook ground beef, onion and garlic until meat is no longer pink, stirring frequently. Drain; transfer to bowl. Toss with Mexican seasoning; set aside.

2. In same skillet over medium heat, sauté rice-vermicelli mix with margarine until vermicelli is golden brown.

3. Slowly stir in 2 cups water, salsa and Special Seasonings; bring to a boil. Cover; reduce heat to low. Simmer 10 minutes.

4. Stir in beef mixture and beans. Cover; simmer 8 to 10 minutes or until rice is tender. Top with cheese.

Makes 6 servings

CURRY BEEF

12 ounces wide egg noodles *or* 1⅓ cups long-grain white rice
1 tablespoon olive oil
1 medium onion, thinly sliced
1 tablespoon curry powder
1 teaspoon ground cumin
2 cloves garlic, minced
1 pound lean ground beef
1 cup (8 ounces) sour cream
½ cup 2% milk
½ cup raisins, divided
1 teaspoon sugar
¼ cup chopped walnuts, almonds or pecans

1. Cook noodles or rice according to package directions. Meanwhile, heat oil in large skillet over medium-high heat until hot. Add onion; cook and stir 3 to 4 minutes. Add curry powder, cumin and garlic; cook 2 to 3 minutes longer or until onion is tender. Add meat; cook 6 to 8 minutes or until meat is no longer pink, breaking meat apart with wooden spoon.

2. Stir in sour cream, milk, ¼ cup raisins and sugar. Reduce heat to medium, stirring constantly, until heated through. Spoon over drained noodles or rice. Sprinkle with remaining ¼ cup raisins and nuts.

Makes 4 servings

Curry Beef

TACO POT PIE

1 pound ground beef
1 package (1.25 ounces) taco
    seasoning mix
¼ cup water
1 can (8 ounces) kidney
    beans, rinsed and
    drained
1 cup chopped tomato
¾ cup frozen corn, thawed
¾ cup frozen peas, thawed
1½ cups (6 ounces) shredded
    Cheddar cheese
1 can (11.5 ounces)
    refrigerated corn
    breadstick dough

1. Preheat oven to 400°F. Brown meat in medium ovenproof skillet over medium-high heat, stirring to separate; drain drippings. Add seasoning mix and water to skillet. Cook over medium-low heat 3 minutes or until most of liquid is absorbed, stirring occasionally.

2. Stir in beans, tomato, corn and peas. Cook 3 minutes or until mixture is hot. Remove from heat; stir in cheese.

3. Unwrap corn bread dough; separate into 16 strips. Twist strips, cutting to fit skillet. Arrange attractively over meat mixture. Press ends of dough lightly to edges of skillet to secure. Bake 15 minutes or until corn bread is golden brown and meat mixture is bubbly.

Makes 4 to 6 servings

Prep and Cook Time:
30 minutes

WESTERN WAGON WHEELS

1 pound lean ground beef or
    ground turkey
2 cups wagon wheel pasta,
    uncooked
1 can (14½ ounces) stewed
    tomatoes
1½ cups water
1 box (10 ounces) BIRDS
    EYE® frozen Sweet Corn
½ cup barbecue sauce
    Salt and pepper to taste

• In large skillet, cook beef over medium heat 5 minutes or until well browned.

• Stir in pasta, tomatoes, water, corn and barbecue sauce; bring to boil.

• Reduce heat to low; cover and simmer 15 to 20 minutes or until pasta is tender, stirring occasionally. Season with salt and pepper. *Makes 4 servings*

Serving Suggestion: Serve with corn bread or corn muffins.

Prep Time: 5 minutes
Cook Time: 25 minutes

Taco Pot Pie

GREATEST SOUPS & STEWS

TEXAS BEEF STEW

1 pound lean ground beef
1 small onion, chopped
1 can (28 ounces) crushed tomatoes with roasted
    garlic
1½ cups BIRDS EYE® frozen Farm Fresh Mixtures
    Broccoli, Cauliflower & Carrots
1 can (14½ ounces) whole new potatoes, halved and
    drained
1 cup BIRDS EYE® frozen Sweet Corn
1 can (4½ ounces) chopped green chilies, drained
½ cup water

• In large saucepan, cook beef and onion over medium-high heat until beef is well browned, stirring occasionally.

• Stir in tomatoes, vegetables, potatoes with liquid, corn, chilies and water; bring to boil.

• Reduce heat to medium-low; cover and simmer
5 minutes or until heated through.

Makes 4 servings

Serving Suggestion: Serve over rice and with warm crusty bread.

Birds Eye Idea: The smell of onions and garlic can penetrate into your cutting boards. Keep a separate cutting board exclusively for these vegetables.

Prep Time: 5 minutes
Cook Time: 15 minutes

CLASSIC MEATBALL SOUP

2 pounds beef bones
3 ribs celery
2 carrots
1 medium onion, cut in half
1 bay leaf
6 cups cold water
1 egg
4 tablespoons chopped fresh
    parsley, divided
1 teaspoon salt, divided
½ teaspoon dried marjoram
    leaves, crushed
¼ teaspoon black pepper,
    divided
½ cup soft fresh bread
    crumbs
¼ cup grated Parmesan
    cheese
1 pound ground beef
1 can (14½ ounces) whole
    peeled tomatoes,
    undrained
½ cup uncooked rotini or
    small macaroni

1. To make stock, rinse bones and combine with celery, carrots, onion and bay leaf in 6-quart stockpot. Add water. Bring to a boil; reduce heat to low. Cover partially and simmer 1 hour, skimming foam occasionally.

2. Preheat oven to 400°F. Spray 13×9-inch baking pan with nonstick cooking spray. Combine egg, 3 tablespoons parsley, ½ teaspoon salt, marjoram and ⅛ teaspoon pepper in medium bowl; whisk lightly. Stir in bread crumbs and cheese. Add beef; mix well. Place meat mixture on cutting board; pat evenly into 1-inch-thick square. With sharp knife, cut meat into 1-inch squares; shape each square into a ball. Place meatballs in prepared pan; bake 20 to 25 minutes until brown on all sides and cooked through, turning occasionally. Drain on paper towels.

3. Strain stock through sieve into medium bowl. Slice celery and carrots; reserve. Discard bones, onion and bay leaf. To degrease stock, let stand 5 minutes to allow fat to rise. Holding paper towel, quickly pull across surface only, allowing towel to absorb fat. Discard. Repeat with clean paper towels as many times as needed to remove all fat.

4. Return stock to stockpot. Drain tomatoes, reserving juice. Chop tomatoes; add to stock with juice. Bring to a boil; boil 5 minutes. Stir in rotini, remaining ½ teaspoon salt and ⅛ teaspoon pepper. Cook 6 minutes, stirring occasionally. Add reserved vegetables and meatballs. Reduce heat to medium; cook 10 minutes until hot. Stir in remaining 1 tablespoon parsley. Season to taste. *Makes 4 to 6 servings*

Classic Meatball Soup

MINESTRONE SOUP WITH MINI MEATBALLS

1 pound ground beef or
    ground turkey
1 teaspoon dried Italian
    seasoning
½ teaspoon garlic powder,
    divided
2 tablespoons vegetable oil,
    divided
5 cups assorted fresh
    vegetables*
1 envelope LIPTON® RECIPE
    SECRETS® Onion Soup
    Mix
4 cups water
1 can (28 ounces) Italian
    plum tomatoes,
    undrained
1 teaspoon sugar

*Use any of the following to equal
5 cups: green beans, cut into 1-inch
pieces, diced zucchini, diced carrot or
diced celery.*

In medium bowl, combine
ground beef, Italian seasoning
and ¼ teaspoon garlic powder.
Shape into 1-inch meatballs.

In 6-quart Dutch oven or heavy
saucepan, heat 1 tablespoon oil
over medium-high heat and
brown meatballs. Remove
meatballs. Heat remaining
1 tablespoon oil in same Dutch
oven and cook vegetables,
stirring frequently, 5 minutes or
until crisp-tender. Stir in soup
mix blended with water,
remaining ¼ teaspoon garlic
powder, tomatoes and sugar.
Bring to a boil over high heat,
breaking up tomatoes with
wooden spoon. Reduce heat to
low and simmer covered
25 minutes. Return meatballs to
skillet. Continue simmering
covered 5 minutes or until
meatballs are heated through.
Serve with grated Parmesan
cheese and garlic bread, if
desired.   *Makes 6 servings*

RAPID RAGÚ® CHILI

1½ pounds lean ground beef
1 medium onion, chopped
2 tablespoons chili powder
1 can (19 ounces) red kidney
    beans, rinsed and
    drained
1 jar (26 to 28 ounces)
    RAGÚ® Old World Style®
    Pasta Sauce
1 cup shredded Cheddar
    cheese (about 4 ounces)

1. In 12-inch skillet, brown
ground beef with onion and chili
powder over medium-high heat,
stirring occasionally. Stir in beans
and Ragú Pasta Sauce.

2. Bring to a boil over high heat.
Reduce heat to low and simmer,
covered, stirring occasionally,
20 minutes. Top with cheese.
Serve, if desired, over hot cooked
rice.   *Makes 6 servings*

Prep Time: 10 minutes
Cook Time: 25 minutes

Rapid Ragú® Chili

FARMER'S STEW ARGENTINA

3 cups water
1 pound lean ground beef
2 tablespoons vegetable oil
1 medium onion, chopped
1 green bell pepper, cut into ½-inch pieces
1 red bell pepper, cut into ½-inch pieces
1 small sweet potato, peeled and cut into ½-inch pieces
1 large clove garlic, minced
1 tablespoon chopped fresh parsley
1 teaspoon salt
½ teaspoon granulated sugar
⅛ teaspoon ground cumin
3 cups beef broth, heated
½ pound zucchini, cut into ½-inch pieces
1 cup whole kernel corn
2 tablespoons raisins
1 teaspoon TABASCO® brand Pepper Sauce
1 small pear, firm but ripe, cut into 1-inch pieces
6 cups cooked white rice

Bring water to a boil in large saucepan. Remove saucepan from heat. Add ground beef, stirring to break meat into little pieces. Let stand 5 minutes, stirring once or twice, until most of the pink disappears from meat. Drain meat well, discarding water.

Heat oil in large deep skillet or Dutch oven over medium-high heat. Add onion and cook 4 to 5 minutes, stirring constantly, until limp and slightly brown.

Add beef. Continue cooking, stirring constantly, until all liquid has evaporated from pan and meat is lightly browned, about 10 minutes.

Reduce heat to medium. Add bell peppers, sweet potato and garlic. Continue cooking and stirring 5 minutes, or until peppers and potatoes are slightly tender. Add parsley, salt, sugar and cumin. Stir and cook 1 minute to blend flavors. Pour beef broth into skillet. Add zucchini, corn, raisins and TABASCO® Sauce. Simmer gently 10 minutes, being careful not to boil. Add pear and simmer 10 additional minutes, or until all fruits and vegetables are tender. Ladle over rice in individual serving bowls.

Makes 6 servings

MEATY CHILI

1 pound coarsely ground
   beef
¼ pound ground Italian
   sausage
1 large onion, chopped
2 medium ribs celery, diced
2 fresh jalapeño peppers,*
   chopped
2 cloves garlic, minced
1 can (28 ounces) whole
   peeled tomatoes,
   undrained, cut up
1 can (15 ounces) pinto
   beans, drained
1 can (12 ounces) tomato
   juice
1 cup water
¼ cup ketchup
1 teaspoon sugar
1 teaspoon chili powder
½ teaspoon salt
½ teaspoon ground cumin
½ teaspoon dried thyme
   leaves
⅛ teaspoon black pepper

*Jalapeño peppers can sting and
irritate the skin; wear rubber gloves
when handling peppers and do not
touch eyes. Wash hands after handling
peppers.

Cook beef, sausage, onion, celery,
jalapeños and garlic in 5-quart
Dutch oven over medium-high
heat until meat is browned and
onion is tender, stirring
frequently.

Stir in tomatoes with juice, beans,
tomato juice, water, ketchup,
sugar, chili powder, salt, cumin,
thyme and black pepper. Bring to
a boil over high heat. Reduce
heat to medium-low; simmer,
uncovered, 30 minutes, stirring
occasionally.

Ladle into bowls. Garnish, if
desired.   *Makes 6 servings*

WILD RICE SOUP

½ cup uncooked wild rice
1 pound lean ground beef
1 can (14½ ounces) chicken
   broth
1 can (10¾ ounces)
   condensed cream of
   mushroom soup
2 cups milk
1 cup (4 ounces) shredded
   Cheddar cheese
⅓ cup shredded carrot
1 packet (.4 ounce) HIDDEN
   VALLEY® The Original
   Ranch® Buttermilk
   Recipe Salad Dressing
   Mix
Chopped green onions with
   tops

Cook rice according to package
directions to make about 1½ cups
cooked rice. In Dutch oven or
large saucepan, brown beef;
drain off excess fat. Stir in rice,
chicken broth, cream of
mushroom soup, milk, cheese,
carrot and dry salad dressing
mix. Heat to a simmer over low
heat, stirring occasionally, about
15 minutes. Serve in warmed
soup bowls; top with green
onions. Garnish with additional
green onions, if desired.
          Makes 6 to 8 servings

RIVERBOAT CHILI

2 pounds lean ground beef
2 large onions, chopped
1 large green pepper,
    chopped
2 cans (14½ ounces each)
    FRANK'S® or
    SNOWFLOSS® Original
    Style Diced Tomatoes,
    undrained
1 can (14½ ounces)
    FRANK'S® or
    SNOWFLOSS® Stewed
    Tomatoes, undrained
⅓ cup MISSISSIPPI®
    Barbecue Sauce
2 bay leaves
3 whole cloves
2 teaspoons chili powder
½ teaspoon cayenne pepper
½ teaspoon paprika
4 cans (15½ ounces each)
    dark red kidney beans

1. Brown ground beef in large stock pot. Drain grease.

2. Add onions, green pepper, diced tomatoes, stewed tomatoes, barbecue sauce, bay leaves, cloves, chili powder, cayenne pepper and paprika. Stir well.

3. Add kidney beans and stir well.

4. Cover and simmer 2 hours, stirring occasionally.
                Makes 4 to 6 servings

Microwave Directions: Crumble beef into large casserole dish. Cook uncovered about 6 minutes stirring at least twice to break up meat. Drain grease. Add onions, green pepper, diced tomatoes,

stewed tomatoes, barbecue sauce, bay leaves, cloves, chili powder, cayenne pepper and paprika. Cook 1 minute. Stir well. Add kidney beans and stir well. Cover and cook 15 to 20 minutes, stirring occasionally. Cover and let stand 5 minutes.

Prep Time: 30 minutes
Cook Time: 2 hours

ALL-IN-ONE BURGER STEW

1 pound lean ground beef
2 cups frozen Italian
    vegetables
1 can (14½ ounces) chopped
    tomatoes with basil and
    garlic, undrained
1 can (about 14 ounces) beef
    broth
2½ cups uncooked medium
    egg noodles
    Salt and black pepper

1. Cook meat in Dutch oven or large skillet over medium-high heat until no longer pink, stirring to separate meat. Drain drippings.

2. Add vegetables, tomatoes with juice and broth; bring to a boil over high heat.

3. Add noodles; reduce heat to medium. Cover and cook 12 to 15 minutes or until noodles have absorbed liquid and vegetables are tender. Add salt and pepper to taste.   *Makes 6 servings*

All-in-One Burger Stew

KANSAS CITY STEAK SOUP

Nonstick cooking spray
½ pound ground sirloin or
  ground round beef
1 cup chopped onion
3 cups frozen mixed
  vegetables·
1 can (14½ ounces) stewed
  tomatoes, undrained
2 cups water
1 cup sliced celery
1 beef bouillon cube
½ to 1 teaspoon black pepper
1 can (10½ ounces) defatted
  beef broth
½ cup all-purpose flour

1. Spray Dutch oven with cooking spray. Heat over medium-high heat until hot. Add beef and onion. Cook and stir 5 minutes or until beef is browned.

2. Add vegetables, tomatoes with juice, water, celery, bouillon cube and pepper. Bring to a boil. Whisk together beef broth and flour until smooth; add to beef mixture, stirring constantly. Return mixture to a boil. Reduce heat to low. Cover and simmer 15 minutes, stirring frequently.

Makes 6 servings

Note: If time permits, allow the soup to simmer an additional 30 minutes—the flavors just get better and better.

BEEFY BROCCOLI & CHEESE SOUP

2 cups chicken broth
1 package (10 ounces) frozen
  chopped broccoli,
  thawed
¼ cup chopped onion
¼ pound ground beef
1 cup milk
2 tablespoons all-purpose
  flour
1 cup (4 ounces) shredded
  sharp Cheddar cheese
1½ teaspoons chopped fresh
  oregano *or* ½ teaspoon
  dried oregano leaves
  Salt and black pepper
  Hot pepper sauce

Bring broth to a boil in medium saucepan. Add broccoli and onion; cook 5 minutes or until broccoli is tender.

Meanwhile, brown ground beef in small skillet; drain. Gradually add milk to flour in small bowl, mixing until well blended. Add with ground beef to broth mixture; cook, stirring constantly, until mixture is thickened and bubbly.

Add cheese and oregano; stir until cheese is melted. Season with salt, pepper and hot pepper sauce to taste.

Makes 4 to 5 servings

Kansas City Steak Soup

IN A FLASH

SALISBURY STEAKS WITH MUSHROOM-WINE SAUCE

1 pound lean ground beef sirloin
¾ teaspoon garlic salt or seasoned salt
¼ teaspoon black pepper
2 tablespoons butter or margarine
1 package (8 ounces) sliced button mushrooms *or*
    2 packages (4 ounces each) sliced exotic
    mushrooms
2 tablespoons sweet vermouth or ruby port wine
1 jar (12 ounces) *or* 1 can (10½ ounces) beef gravy

1. Heat large heavy nonstick skillet over medium-high heat 3 minutes or until hot.* Meanwhile, combine ground sirloin, garlic salt and pepper; mix well. Shape mixture into four ¼-inch-thick oval patties.

2. Place patties in skillet as they are formed; cook 3 minutes per side or until browned. Transfer to plate. Pour off drippings.

3. Melt butter in skillet; add mushrooms. Cook and stir 2 minutes. Add vermouth; cook 1 minute. Add gravy; mix well.

4. Return patties to skillet; simmer, uncovered, over medium heat 2 minutes for medium or until desired doneness, turning meat and stirring sauce.

Makes 4 servings

If pan is not heavy, use medium heat.

Note: For a special touch, sprinkle steaks with chopped parsley or chives.

CRUNCHY LAYERED BEEF & BEAN SALAD

1 pound ground beef or turkey
2 cans (15 to 19 ounces *each*) black beans or pinto beans, rinsed and drained
1 can (14½ ounces) stewed tomatoes, undrained
1½ cups *French's*® French Fried Onions, divided
1 tablespoon *Frank's*® *RedHot*® Cayenne Pepper Sauce
1 package (1¼ ounces) taco seasoning mix
6 cups shredded lettuce
1 cup (4 ounces) shredded Cheddar or Monterey Jack cheese

1. Cook beef in large nonstick skillet over medium heat until thoroughly browned; drain well. Stir in beans, tomatoes, *⅔ cup* French Fried Onions, *Frank's RedHot* Sauce and taco seasoning. Heat to boiling. Cook over medium heat 5 minutes, stirring occasionally.

2. Spoon beef mixture over lettuce on serving platter. Top with cheese.

3. Microwave remaining *1 cup* onions 1 minute on HIGH. Sprinkle over salad.

Makes 6 servings

Prep Time: 10 minutes
Cook Time: 6 minutes

SONOMA BURGERS STUFFED WITH BLUE CHEESE

½ pound ground beef or meat of your choice
Salt and pepper
1 tablespoon Worcestershire sauce
2 ounces blue cheese, divided
8 SONOMA® Marinated Tomatoes, chopped
½ medium yellow onion, finely chopped

Season meat lightly with salt and pepper. Mix in Worcestershire sauce; halve the meat mixture and form into two patties. Carve a cavity into the center of each patty and stuff with blue cheese. Set aside.

Heat a non-stick skillet over medium-high heat until hot. Heat marinated tomatoes with some of their oil and the onion until mixture sizzles. Push mixture aside and add the two patties; let meat sear to seal in juices, then reduce heat to medium. Cover pan and let cook 2 to 2½ minutes on each side. Add a pinch more of salt and pepper during last minutes of cooking. Serve each burger on toasted bread, if desired. Garnish with tomatoes and onions.

Makes 2 servings

Prep Time: 5 minutes
Cooking Time: 8 minutes

Crunchy Layered Beef & Bean Salad

FAST 'N EASY CHILI

1½ pounds ground beef
1 envelope LIPTON® RECIPE
  SECRETS® Onion Soup
  Mix*
1 can (15 to 19 ounces) red
  kidney or black beans,
  drained
1½ cups water
1 can (8 ounces) tomato
  sauce
4 teaspoons chili powder

*Also terrific with LIPTON® RECIPE
SECRETS® Beefy Mushroom, Onion-
Mushroom or Beefy Onion Soup Mix.*

1. In 12-inch skillet, brown
ground beef over medium-high
heat; drain.

2. Stir in remaining ingredients.
Bring to a boil over high heat.
Reduce heat to low and simmer
covered, stirring occasionally,
20 minutes. Top hot chili with
shredded Cheddar cheese, and
serve over hot cooked rice, if
desired.   *Makes 6 servings*

First Alarm Chili: Add
5 teaspoons chili powder.

Second Alarm Chili: Add
2 tablespoons chili powder.

Third Alarm Chili: Add chili
powder at your own risk.

CREAMY BEEF AND VEGETABLE CASSEROLE

1 pound lean ground beef
1 small onion, chopped
1 bag (16 ounces) BIRDS
  EYE® frozen Farm Fresh
  Mixtures Broccoli, Corn
  & Red Peppers
1 can (10¾ ounces) cream of
  mushroom soup

• In medium skillet, brown beef
and onion; drain excess fat.

• Meanwhile, in large saucepan,
cook vegetables according to
package directions; drain.

• Stir in beef mixture and soup.
Cook over medium heat until
heated through.
          Makes 4 servings

Serving Suggestion: Serve over
rice and sprinkle with ½ cup
shredded Cheddar cheese.

Prep Time: 5 minutes
Cook Time: 10 to 15 minutes

SLOPPY JOE ROLLERS

1 small onion, finely chopped
¼ cup finely chopped red bell
    pepper
1½ pounds ground beef
¾ cup chili sauce
2 tablespoons *French's®*
    Worcestershire Sauce
1⅓ cups *French's®* French
    Fried Onions
1 cup shredded Cheddar
    cheese
8 (10-inch) flour tortillas,
    heated

1. Heat *1 tablespoon oil* in 12-inch nonstick skillet over medium-high heat. Cook onion and red pepper 2 minutes. Stir in meat and cook 5 minutes or until browned; drain. Stir in chili sauce and Worcestershire. Simmer 3 minutes.

2. To serve, arrange meat mixture, French Fried Onions and cheese down center of tortillas, dividing evenly. Fold bottom third of each tortilla over filling; fold sides towards center. Tightly roll up to secure filling. Cut in half to serve.

Makes 8 servings

Prep Time: 5 minutes
Cook Time: 10 minutes

QUICK 'N' EASY TACOS

1 pound ground beef
1 can (14½ ounces) whole
    peeled tomatoes,
    undrained and coarsely
    chopped
1 medium green bell pepper,
    finely chopped
1 envelope LIPTON® RECIPE
    SECRETS® Onion Soup
    Mix*
1 tablespoon chili powder
3 drops hot pepper sauce
    (optional)
8 taco shells
    Taco Toppings

*Also terrific with Lipton® Recipe Secrets® Onion-Mushroom or Beefy Mushroom Soup Mix.

In medium skillet, brown ground beef over medium-high heat; drain. Stir in tomatoes, green pepper, onion soup mix, chili powder and hot pepper sauce. Bring to a boil, then simmer 15 minutes or until slightly thickened. Serve in taco shells with assorted Taco Toppings.

Makes 4 servings

Taco Toppings: Use shredded Cheddar or Monterey Jack cheese, shredded lettuce, chopped tomatoes, sliced pitted ripe olives, sour cream or taco sauce.

SWEET AND SOUR BEEF

1 pound lean ground beef
1 small onion, thinly sliced
2 teaspoons minced fresh
    ginger
1 package (16 ounces) frozen
    mixed vegetables (snap
    peas, carrots, water
    chestnuts, pineapple, red
    pepper
6 to 8 tablespoons bottled
    sweet and sour sauce or
    sauce from vegetable mix
Cooked rice

1. Place meat, onion and ginger
in large skillet; cook over high
heat 6 to 8 minutes or until no
longer pink, breaking apart with
wooden spoon. Pour off
drippings.

2. Stir in frozen vegetables and
sauce. Cook, covered, 6 to
8 minutes, stirring every
2 minutes or until vegetables are
heated through. Serve over rice.
Makes 4 servings

Serving Suggestion: Serve with
sliced Asian apple-pears.

Prep and Cook Time:
15 minutes

GROOVY ANGEL HAIR GOULASH

1 pound lean ground beef
2 tablespoons margarine or
    butter
1 (4.8-ounce) package
    PASTA RONI® Angel Hair
    Pasta with Herbs
1 (14½-ounce) can diced
    tomatoes, undrained
1 cup frozen or canned corn,
    drained

1. In large skillet over medium-
high heat, brown ground beef.
Remove from skillet; drain. Set
aside.

2. In same skillet, bring 1½ cups
water and margarine to a boil.

3. Stir in pasta; cook 1 minute
or just until pasta softens slightly.
Stir in tomatoes, corn, beef and
Special Seasonings; return to a
boil. Reduce heat to medium.
Gently boil uncovered, 4 to
5 minutes or until pasta is tender,
stirring frequently. Let stand 3 to
5 minutes before serving.
Makes 4 servings

Prep Time: 5 minutes
Cook Time: 15 minutes

Sweet and Sour Beef

SPEEDY BEEF & BEAN BURRITOS

8 flour tortillas (7-inch)
1 pound ground beef
1 cup chopped onion
1 teaspoon bottled minced
    garlic
1 can (15 ounces) black
    beans, drained and
    rinsed
1 cup spicy thick and chunky
    salsa
2 teaspoons ground cumin
1 bunch cilantro
2 cups (8 ounces) shredded
    cojack or Monterey Jack
    cheese

1. Wrap tortillas in foil; place on center rack in oven. Heat oven to 350°F; heat tortillas 15 minutes.

2. While tortillas are warming, prepare burrito filling. Combine beef, onion and garlic in large skillet; cook over medium-high heat until beef is no longer pink, breaking beef apart with wooden spoon. Pour off drippings.

3. Stir beans, salsa and cumin into beef mixture; reduce heat to medium. Cover and simmer 10 minutes, stirring once.

4. While filling is simmering, chop enough cilantro to measure ¼ cup. Stir into filling. Spoon filling down centers of warm tortillas; top with cheese. Roll up and serve immediately.
Makes 4 servings

Prep and Cook Time:
20 minutes

BISTRO BURGERS WITH BLUE CHEESE

1 pound ground turkey or
    beef
¼ cup chopped fresh parsley
2 tablespoons minced chives
¼ teaspoon dried thyme
    leaves
2 tablespoons *French's®* Napa
    Valley Style Dijon
    Mustard
    Lettuce and tomato slices
4 crusty rolls, split in half
2 ounces blue cheese,
    crumbled
1⅓ cups *French's®* French
    Fried Onions

1. In large bowl, gently mix meat, herbs and mustard. Shape into 4 patties.

2. Grill or broil patties 10 minutes or until no longer pink in center. Arrange lettuce and tomatoes on bottom half of rolls. Place burgers on top. Sprinkle with blue cheese and French Fried Onions. Cover with top half of rolls. Serve with additional mustard.

Tip: Toast onions in microwave 1 minute for extra crispness.
Makes 4 servings

Prep Time: 10 minutes
Cook Time: 10 minutes

Speedy Beef &
Bean Burritos

The publisher would like to thank the companies and organizations listed below for the use of their recipes and photographs in this publication.

Barilla America, Inc.

Birds Eye®

Del Monte Corporation

The Fremont Company, Makers of Frank's & SnowFloss Kraut & Mississippi BBQ Sauce

The Golden Grain Company®

The Hidden Valley® Food Products Company

McIlhenny Company (TABASCO® brand Pepper Sauce)

North Dakota Beef Commission

North Dakota Wheat Commission

The Quaker® Oatmeal Kitchens

Reckitt Benckiser Inc.

Riviana Foods Inc.

Sonoma® Dried Tomatoes

Uncle Ben's Inc.

Unilever Bestfoods North America

USA Dry Pea & Lentil Council

Wisconsin Milk Marketing Board

✯✯✯ INDEX ✯✯✯